God commands us to be strong.

His Word says to put on His armour.

We should wear it daily.

© 2020 Chelsea Kong

All rights reserved. All images used in this book are licensed copies from their respectful owners including Freepik, and myself. This book or any portion thereof may not be reproduced or used in any manner whatsoever without the express written permission of the publisher except for the use of brief quotations in a book review.

Printed in 2020, Made in Toronto, Canada

ARMOUR of GOD

Chelsea Kong

What is the Armour of God?

It's just like a knight wearing armour.

God's armour is not seen with our regular eyes.

The armour we wear keeps us from the devil's attacks.

God tells us to put on the full armour and we are to keep it on (Ephesians 6:10-13).

What God Word says

So, stand strong, with the belt of truth tied around your waist. And on your chest wear the protection of right living. And on your feet wear the Good News of peace to help you stand strong. And also use the shield of faith. With that you can stop all the burning arrows of the Evil One. Accept God's salvation to be your helmet. And take the sword of the Spirit; that sword is the teaching of God. Pray in the Spirit at all times. Pray with all kinds of prayers, and ask for everything you need. To do this you must always be ready. Never give up. Always pray for all God's people. (Ephesians 6:14-18)

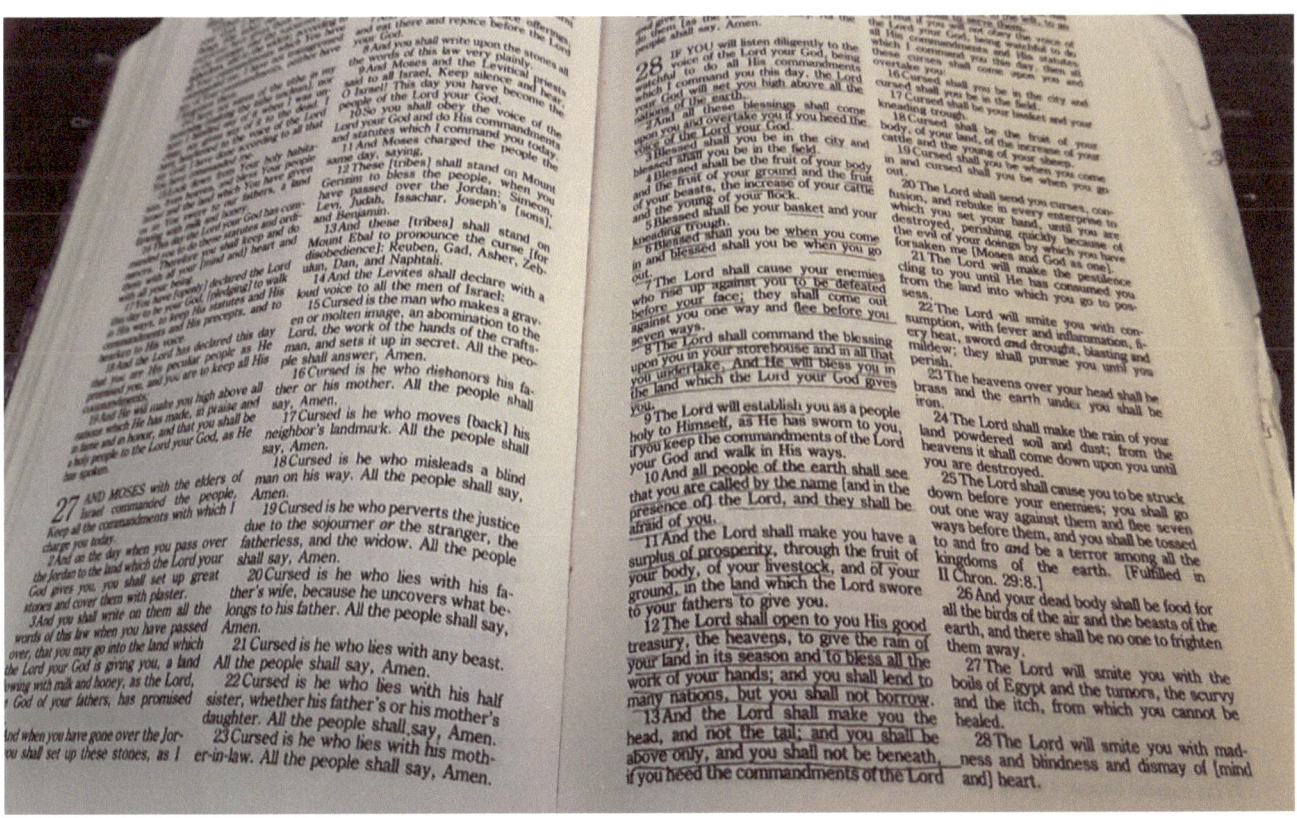

The fight is against the unseen

Our fight is not against people on earth. We are fighting against the rulers and authorities and the powers of this world's darkness. We are fighting against the spiritual powers of evil in the heavenly world. (Ephesians 6:12)

Why do I need it?

That is why you need to get God's full armor. Then on the day of evil you will be able to stand strong. And when you have finished the whole fight, you will still be standing. (Ephesians 6:13)

Belt of Truth

God's Word is the Truth that protects us from evil.

The Truth can attack back to destroy the lies.

We become strong in knowing who we are in God and what Jesus has done for us.

Breastplate/Chest Wear

It protects us to live in the right way.

It keeps us from living on the wrong path.

The chest wear keeps us walking a pure and clean life.

Shoes for your feet

It brings good news that Jesus Christ died on the cross and rose from the dead to give us new life forever.

It keeps our feet firm to stand and walk in God's ways.

It lets us walk in God's love, peace, and joy.

Shield of Faith

It stops the enemy's attacks he does to us.

The faith of God keeps away all doubt and fear.

It stops evil from touching us.

Faith lets us receive from God and be close to Him.

Helmet of Salvation

God saved us and our mind needs to be changed.

It protects our minds away from the wrong thoughts and pictures that the enemy gives us.

Jesus gave us new life in Him and all that we need.

We have health, blessing, more than enough, freedom, and many more things from God.

Sword of the Spirit

It is the **Word** of **God** and the power of the **Holy Spirit**.

It has the power to destroy the evil one's attacks.

God's power can divide.

It is a double-sided sword.

Pray in the Holy Spirit

Pray in the power of the Holy Spirit.

Pray in the language He gives.

Pray as He leads.

Pray all the time.

All kinds of Prayers

Pray for others and yourself.

Pray for protection.

Pray against the enemy.

Pray for everything you need.

Types of Prayers

1. **B**lessing and **A**doration (Worship)
2. **P**etition (asking for something asking for favour)
3. Intercession (for others)
4. Thanksgiving
5. Praise

Worship

Worship God for who He is.

Do it in spirit and truth.

Allow yourself to show how much you love Him.

You can dance, sing, and wait for Him.

Asking

Ask, Seek, and Knock and the door will be opened to you.

Ask God with a clean heart of love.

See Him and think about Him.

Pray for Others

God's Word said to pray for others all the time.

Pray for kings and leaders, leaders also in Church, and all those who God put over you.

Always be ready to pray and never give up.

Pray for the Good news to be shared with everyone.

Giving Thanks

Be thankful all the time for all things.

It opens the way for God to work and give us what we asked.

We can make the things we don't have yet show up.

Praise

God will stay with us when we praise.

It attracts God to answer our prayer.

It changes the place where we are.

Salvation Prayer

God, I know that I have sinned against you. Forgive me for the wrong that I have done. I believe that Jesus Christ died on the cross for me and that He rose from the grave after three days. That I can have His long-lasting life. Come into my heart to be my Lord and Savior. I choose to turn away from the wrong I did and choose to follow you. Lead me to walk with you. Keep me safe and teach me your ways. Stop every bad thing in my life that has an open door to hurt me. Close those doors. Holy Spirit fill me now in Jesus' name. Amen.

Baptism in the Holy Spirit

Jesus, you are the one that fills me with Your Spirit. Come Holy Spirit and come into my life and fill me to overflow with Your presence. Come with your fire too. Thank you for the gift of tongues in Jesus' name. Amen.

Open your mouth and let the words come out that God gives you. It will be words that you don't know what they mean. God can give you the meaning when you ask Him. Keep giving God your mouth to speak it out. You need to let Him talk through you every day to grow this gift. He will also take you closer to God and you will know more about Jesus and have power from God to do great things and know things.

Prayer

Father God, thank you for your armour to protect us from the evil one. That I would remain in the Truth and speak Your Word only. That you keep me in perfect love, peace, joy, and hope. Jesus, teach me how to share the good news with others. Holy Spirit keeps me in the right way and always prays at all times. To keep in faith, stay close to You, and stand strong in Jesus' name. Amen.

Message from the Author

God's armour is the only way to protect us from evil. We need to keep watch over the words we speak and the thoughts and pictures that come to mind. Use God's Word all the time when the evil one attacks us. It has the power to divide and destroy doubts and fear. We need to keep our eyes on Jesus, think, and see Him with us. We need to keep the bad out of our lives. The more we pray by the Holy Spirit the stronger we become and it makes us closer to God. He will show us things that will keep us safe. It will bless us.

Other Products

Knowing God
How to Hear God's Voice
New Life in Jesus
Loving Israel
God's Gifts
Meeting God
Word Power
Fruit of the Spirit
The Tabernacle
Bride for Jesus
A Life of Prayer
Live Free
Who am I in Jesus
Walk in Love
God's Favor
Man of God
Woman of God
How to Use Money
God's Wisdom
Fasting
See Jerusalem and Bethany
First Fruit Offering
Feast of Trumpets
Day of Atonement
Feast of Tabernacles
Counting the Omer
Festival of Lights
Glory, Presence, and Holy Spirit
Live in God's Presence

31 Day Devotional
Biblical Puzzle Book Vol 1
Biblical Puzzle Book Vol 2
Biblical Puzzle Book Vol 4
Biblical Puzzle Book Vol 5

Teaching (Non-Sale)
Purim
Passover
Resurrection

Bible Puzzles for Young Children Book 1
Bible Puzzles for Young Children Book 2
Bible Puzzles for Young Children Book 3

How God Speaks
Knowing Jesus
Knowing Holy Spirit

Teaching Series
How to Hear God's Voice Teaching Guide & Audio Book
Relationship with God, Jesus, Holy Spirit Guide
Knowing God, Jesus, Holy Spirit Guide & Audio Book

More books on Amazon, Kobo, and Barnes and Noble
Check out the teaching series on her website:

https://chelseak532002550.wordpress.com/

Chelsea Kong's Biography

She is a writer, creative arts and digital media artist, and skilled administrative professional. She also served in a variety of roles from audiovisual, photography, to assisting on the worship team, and ministry team. She is also has a passion for families being united. Her writing consists of children's books, stories, bridal writing, poems, lyrics for songs, words of encouragement, blessings, prayers, and jokes. She is the author of the **Bridal Collection, Knowing God, How to Hear God's Voice, New Life in Jesus, Loving Israel, God's Gifts, Meeting God, Word Power, Fruit of the Spirit, The Tabernacle, Bride for Jesus, A Life of Prayer**, etc. She also has her own **Bible Puzzle** books and other inspired products. She also has her own 31 days devotional and other inspired products. Her podcast channel on self-development is called Chelsea K on Anchor, Spotify, iTunes, etc. Her podcasts can also be found on YouTube. Chelsea has been on Unity Live Radio and The Lady Tracey Show. She has published an article on Woman of God on ReadersMagnet in Author Lounge and has good reviews on her books. She has more opportunities coming soon.

The Armour of God is our protection against the invisible enemy!

The weapons of our warfare are spiritual. We need God's protection to fight the good fight of fight. Learn how to put on your armour and fight with His Word. It is God's will for us to stay under His protection against the enemy. We can only this if we have the armour of God. Know what the armour of God is and the benefits of having it. This book will teach your child or children each part of the armour and how it is used to protect us. Angels are always watching over us, but it is our role to command them to work for us.

2019 Copyright Chelsea Kong and respected owners. All rights reserved.

www.ingramcontent.com/pod-product-compliance
Lightning Source LLC
Chambersburg PA
CBHW041416010526
44107CB00016B/1194